BASICS
FOR BEGINNERS

Oliver & Harald Olsen & Valery Niazov

Balboa Press books may be ordered through booksellers or by contacting:

Balboa Press
A Division of Hay House
1663 Liberty Drive
Bloomington, IN 47403
www.balboapress.com
1 (877) 407-4847

Because of the dynamic nature of the Internet, any web addresses or links contained in this book may have changed since publication and may no longer be valid. The views expressed in this work are solely those of the author and do not necessarily reflect the views of the publisher, and the publisher hereby disclaims any responsibility for them.

Any people depicted in stock imagery provided by Thinkstock are models, and such images are being used for illustrative purposes only.
Certain stock imagery © Thinkstock.

ISBN: 978-1-5043-1102-1 (sc)
ISBN: 978-1-5043-1103-8 (e)

Print information available on the last page.

Balboa Press rev. date: 06/27/2018

BALBOA
PRESS
A DIVISION OF HAY HOUSE

INTRODUCTION

The martial arts are ultimately self-knowledge. A punch or a kick is not to knock the hell out of the guy in front, but to knock the hell out of your ego, your fear, or your hang-ups.

Bruce Lee

Muay Thai (MT) is a centuries old fighting system born in Thailand. It offers an enjoyable fitness system that combines cardio, endurance, strength and conditioning exercises with a development of cognitive skills. It enhances concentration and builds a strong and balanced mind.

Others find in Muay Thai a thrill of a combat and a test of one's skills. All Muay Thai practitioners appreciate and maintain the environment of mutual respect, humility and camaraderie in Muay Thai gyms. Because of its versatility, this sport is accessible to any person at any age and gender. Not surprisingly, Muay Thai is becoming popular around the world and some of its techniques are also used by MMA fighters.

This book is for beginners. The detailed explanations of Muay Thai basic techniques are provided by two renowned Australian Muay Thai fighters/coaches; cousins Oliver and Harald Olsen who have over 60 years of experience in the ring.

If you are considering joining a Muay Thai gym or you are beginning your Muay Thai journey this book will help you to develop your skills. Good luck and enjoy! The book is easy to read, understand and practice.

ABOUT THE PEOPLE WHO WILL GUIDE YOU ON THIS JOURNEY

Oliver Olsen

Oliver's rise to fame as a fighter was launched in 1993 when he won his first State title by defeating Australian boxing legend Danny Green. He subsequently won four more State titles, two Australian National titles with KOs against legendary Queensland fighter Tony Hill and kick boxing World Champion Steve Duet. Among Oliver's achievements are a Bronze Medal in the 1999 Armature games during which he won four out of five fights by KO and the World Muay Thai (WMTA) title in 1999.

He started his coaching career in 1996. In 2009 he opened his gym, Olsen Muay Thai Factory, in Perth. The gym quickly became one of the most popular Muay Thai fighting gyms producing many outstanding champions like Troy Heygate, Kaitlyn Vance, Marc Gibbons, Alana Neal, Tim Mitchell, Roy Daynes, Marc Abonetti, Jackson Moorehouse to name a few.

Today Oliver continues to train and nurture future fighters as well as people who simply love Muay Thai to stay healthy and fit. Oliver's gym, however, is also renowned for its environment of mutual assistance and respect among many people of different age, gender and cultures. This is a manifestation of Oliver's personality and his standing among the martial arts community of Australia.

Harald Olsen

With over 30 years of international and Australian Muay Thai fight experiences, with numerous titles under his belt and a practical knowledge of different martial arts, Harald is considered by many Muay Thai fighters as an expert on different aspects of training, fitness and fight strategies and preparations. In 2017 at the age of 46, Harald retired from fighting and opened his own gym - House of Olsen -Muay Thai Noble Falls -Gidgegannup gym.

NOTE

The book is the result of interviews with Oliver and Harald Olsen by Valery Niazov.

Photography for this book is taken by Ming Eu Olsen.

The authors would like to point out that all techniques suggested in the book are based on Oliver's and Harald's many years of coaching and fighting experiences. Different fighters and coaches use different approaches to training.

CHAPTER I

BASIC FOOT WORK AND STANCE

Foot work is fundamental for a balanced movement and it is paramount for a beginner to understand and master it.

The following stance can be adopted by beginners:

- The *Lead Foot* is positioned at around 11 - 12 o'clock (this position will also allow you to quickly block an inside or outside kick from your opponent). Remember that the good fighters will see the position of your legs and will attack accordingly.

Pic 3   Pic 4

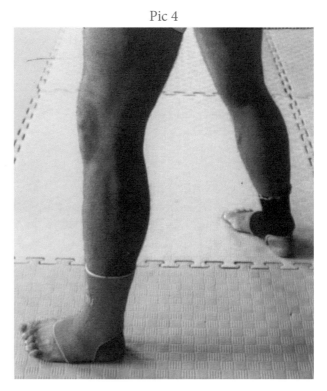

- The *Back Foot* is positioned diagonally from your *Lead Foot* at 2 o'clock angle.
- The distance between the two feet is approximately 30-40 cm. You don't want the distance between your feet to be too narrow because you will have a weak base and hence no power. But neither do you want the distance between your feet to be too wide because it prevents you from being mobile.
- Your legs should be slightly bent.
- The body weight is placed equally on two legs with the central point in between.

During sparing or a fight you can use:

- Defensive Stance.

  In this position, your Lead Foot is on the ball of the foot, and your weight is placed on the Back Foot in a flat position. This allows you to react faster with your shin to defend a kick from your opponent and maintain good balance.

pic 6

- Offence Stance. Use this stance when you are about to launch an attack. In this position the Back Foot is kept on its ball to enable a swift movement.

Pic 7

Practice standing in the correct position on the floor.

Practice shifting weights in between two positions Defense and Offence.

How to hold your hands correctly in a Stance-Guard position

The purpose of this position is obviously to protect yourself from your opponent's strikes. There are many different guard positions.

- In full Muay Thai rules, the hands are usually kept up high to protect against your opponent's elbows as well as punches.
- The elbows should be kept a little away from your body so that you can protect your body and even damage your opponent's leg when it connects with your elbow.

For a conventional **Stance-Guard** position:

- Hide your chin behind your left shoulder (pic8). Bend the left elbow but keep your arm a little forward under 45 degrees.
- Place your right hand at your temple (pic 9). See pic 10-12 for different variations of the Stance-Guard position.

8

9

10

11

12

The second position is called **Peek-a-boo:**

- Place your two fists to your forehead. Keep your thumbs above eyebrows as if you are looking through your guard (pic 13)
- Keep your both shoulders rolled in and your two arms close to your body with your elbows tucked in to protect the ribs.
- When your opponent strikes, you can squeeze the gloves to your temple so that your Guard position is strong.

Pic13   pic 14

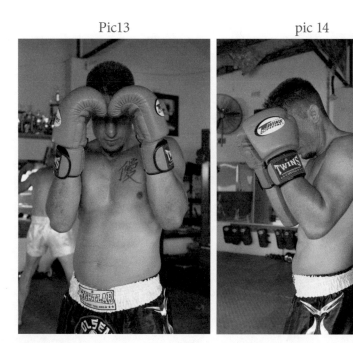

Pic15

Tip: Practice the *Guard* and the *Picaboo* positions in front of the mirror.

How to move forward and back, circle and pivot to make angles

Once you learn the correct *Stance* and foot positioning, start practicing moving forward and backwards. During the movement pay attention to your feet positioning, correct stance and hand positioning.

Below is a breakdown of a basic move forward:

- *Back Foot* generates the move but it is the *Lead Foot* that moves forward first.
- Then the *Back Foot* drags to position.

Pic`16   17   18

- When you move forward the steps should not be bigger then 25-30 cm. However, it depends on your opponent's fighting style (defensive or offensive).
- When you move, try not to be flat on your feet but keep them on their balls. This will also enable you to quickly re-adjust your position etc.
- You can also use short steps which will make you quicker and lighter on your feet.

Moving backwards with the *Back Foot* stepping first.

Balanced foot work makes a better fighter. One way to maintain balance while you constantly move is to keep on the balls of your feet. It is not easy, but it will become comfortable with more training.

Practice tips:

Remember to always bring yourself into balance during the movement, by adjusting with little steps.

To practice the foot work, place an object on the floor. Move with two steps towards the object, then move back with two steps. Practice until your movement is smooth and flowing. Remember always to keep the correct position (feet, legs and the guard).

Pivoting

It is important to stay mobile and keep moving around the ring during sparring or a fight.

Pivoting is one technique used for avoiding your opponent's attack while using it as a transition for a strike or a kick from a different angle. Hence pivoting is used for offence and defence to create angles and opportunities for counter-strikes or own attacks.

To pivot,

- With your *Leading Foot,* step aside and away from your opponent's frontal attack.
- Then move across with the other foot. In this way, you are positioning yourself to the side of your opponent. Then you can retaliate with a kick, cross or a hook.

Follow the diagram below:

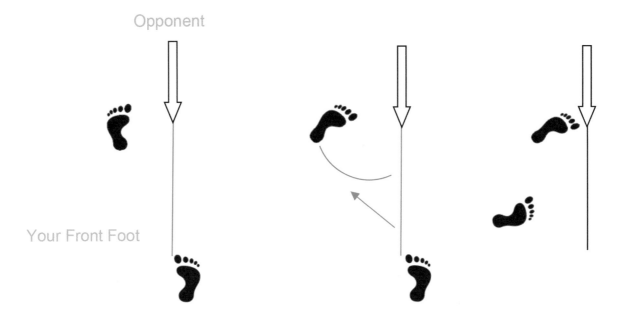

Practice pivoting

- Moving forward then stepping 45-degrees away from the frontal line of the attack and performing a pivot.
- Go back to the original position and repeat the pivot.
- Practice the pivot as part of your training.

Side to Side movement

This movement is particularly used by fighters when their back is against the ropes and they want to move away from the attack and move back to the centre of the ring.

Practice it by starting off in a proper *Stance/Guard* position (legs, feet, arms).

- To move left, step with your *Lead Foot* first, then follow with your *Back Foot*.
- Square your stance and move your legs from side to side. An example is a basketball defense.

SUGGESTED DRILL

- Perform a Full Circle movement in one direction and once the circle is concluded immediately circle into the opposite direction. Finish at the original position.
- Combine movements: forward, backwards, pivoting and circling.
- Repeat, repeat, repeat perfecting the balance of the foot work and the drill.

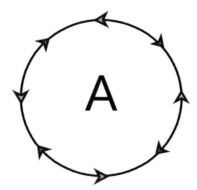

- After completing a full circle start circling in the opposite direction. Whilst circling, look at the center point (A).

21

22

23

24-

25

CHAPTER II
BASIC STRIKIES

There are four basic hand strikes; jab, cross, hook and uppercut. Depending on the distance, angle etc, fighters use many different striking techniques. You should use a technique taught to you by your coach.

Note that all strikes involve a compound movement utilizing your feet, legs, knees, hips and shoulders. The point of contact is the result of these parts working together.

1. Jab

- Assume a stance as described in the previous chapter.
- Keep your guard up protecting yourself.
- The jab is generated by the *Lead Foot* stepping forward.
- Use your hips and shoulders to shoot your lead hand towards your opponent's face
- Slightly twist the knuckles of your fist on impact.

Harald is in South Paw Stance

| 26 | 27 | 28 |

Oli in Orthodox Stance

Tip: stepping and jabbing should constitute one movement. There is no need for real power.

- Practice stepping forward and back as described in the previous chapter but add the jab.

Tip: An ineffective strike is the result of insufficient balance caused by you leaning forward to reach your opponent because you are too far from the opponent. In this position, you also leave yourself open to an attack from your opponent. Therefore, to cover more distance use two steps doubled up with jabs.

- WRONG FORM

- INAFFICENT

Practice tips:

- Practice jabs in front of the mirror
- Practice step and jab in front of the mirror
- Practice moving forward and backwards throwing jabs

2. Cross

Cross is a power strike with your strong hand. As a movement, it has several components:

- Power is generated by the Back Leg which pivots on the ball of the Foot (from 2 to 12 o'clock position). Pic 34-35
- *Right Shoulder* thrust forward while the left is thrusting in opposite direction.
- Lead arm strikes.
- All components are one movement.

| 34 | 35 | 36 | 37 |

PRACTICE:

- practice cross in front of the mirror
- practice moving forward and backwards and crossing
- practice moving forward and backwards adding jabs and crosses

TIP:

When attacking by going forward use the following movement: step – step – quick stop (to balance your base) followed by a cross. The power is generating from your body.

When you deliver a cross, keep your eyes on the opponent. Tuck your chin in to your right shoulder whilst your left hand protects the side of your head (pic 36). Upon the impact turn your knuckles and the wrist slightly with a downward movement to increase power.

3. Left Hook

A Hook is delivered by the three parts of your body working together: legs, hips, shoulder/arm.

To deliver a *Hook*:

- Slightly twist your upper body to the left (pic 36). Do not pull back your left arm and immediately spring it to the right to deliver a left hook. Do the opposite for the right hook.
- The *Lead Foot* and the knee twists to 2 o'clock position with the knee aligned with your toes. (Pic 39)
- The power is generated by the *Lead Leg* then it transfers through the hip then the shoulder thrusting in the same direction. The movement ends in the hook.
- The elbow should be on the same level as the hand.

Practice: throw a cross and follow with the left hook

4. Right Hook

- Use the three parts of your body working together: legs, hips, shoulder/arm.
- *Right Hook* springs from the Stance/Guard position.
- Slightly twist your upper body to the right and immediately spring it to the left to deliver a right hook.
- Return to Stance/ Guard position.

Harald demonstrated Right Hook

Some prefer to keep their wrist with the palm almost facing down.

PRACTICE

- Jab, cross, hook in stationary position
- Practice jab, cross, hook while moving forward and backwards

5. Uppercut

The compound movement principles described earlier also apply for uppercuts.

- To deliver an upper cut, you should drop the shoulder or slightly twist your body down. (Pic 48 & 52)
- Power is generated and transferred from your *Back Foot* through the *Back Leg*, hip, body and finally the Uppercut. (Pic 50 & 53)

54

55

56

57

58

Practice uppercuts in front of the mirror and on a bag, then add a combination consisting of uppercuts and hooks.

6. Forward UP Elbow

The compound movement for the up elbow strike is similar as for the uppercut. The power is generated by the velocity coming from the step combined with the short burst of the hip and the power of the body.

The elbow can be aimed in between the guards when it strikes up.

Practice in a stationary position: Lead and Back elbows, then practice on pads with your partner.

7. Right Down Elbow -

To practice:

- From your Stance, your striking elbow moves up and horizontal to the floor. The palm is facing towards your opponent. (Pic 65)
- Your other hand is in a guard position.
- Your striking elbow should be moving forward and down.

TIP: The power is generated by your body weight plus velocity. Don't over rotate your elbow or it will affect your balance, it will also leave you open for a counter strike.

Lead Elbow

64   65   66

Back Elbow

67   68   69

8. Round House (RH) kick

RH kick is the most common kick in Muay Thai for attacking your opponent with power.

The most common targets of the RH kick are:

- Side of the body, ribs, liver and arms – (Middle Kick).
- The RH kick can be used to target your opponent's head – (head Kick)

Like in all previous strikes the compound movement plays an important role in generating the power to deliver a kick.

It consists of:

- Stepping forward slightly to the right or left side of your opponent, with your *Lead Foot* moving to 10 or 2 o'clock position.
- The power is generated through the rolling hip of the kicking leg.
- When kicking with the *Right Leg* your right shoulder and the arm move in opposite direction of the kick (pics 4 &12 below). Your left hand should be in a guard position on delivery of the kick (pic 4).
- When kicking with your *Left Leg* the Right Hand should be in a guard position (pics 10 &13) to protect yourself from your opponent's punches.

TIPS

- You should practice the RH kick first slowly, without power, trying to understand the movement and get the correct technique.
- Place your straight leg on an object (e.g.: a table; the height depends on your flexibility). Then turn your hips and your knee towards the imaginary target. Also note the movement of your hands (described above).
- Once you are comfortable, start kicking a bag. First kicking it softly and focusing on the movement
- Then adding the power and finally speed and power.

In the second book, *Advanced Technique for Fighters*, we will talk about switching technique.

70

71

72

73

74

75

76

77

78

Low Kick

Low kick is aimed at the quads, outer or inner thighs of your opponent.

80

81

82

9. Step up Knee strikes

Knee strikes can be delivered in the following manner:

- From your Stance Position, step forward strike with your knee. Your toes are pointing down, (Pic 86)
- For better balance keep your supporting leg on the ball of the foot.
- Lean your upper body back when the knee collides with the target. (pic 87)
- Upon the contact thrust and rotate your hip into your opponent to get more power. (pic 87)

Practice:

- Once you are comfortable start kneeing a bag. First do it softly, focusing on the movement.
- Then adding the power and finally - speed and power.
- You also can practice by alternating right and left knees strikes.
- Another way to practice knee strikes is to move forward on the floor striking alternatively with right and left knee.

TIP: You can add the first combination: jab-cross –right knee- right RH kick

10. Push Kick

There are two types of push kicks: Back Leg Push Kick and Front Leg Push Kick. The first is used for offence and the latter is used for defence.

The *Back-Leg Push Kick* technique can be described as following:

- Stand in a Stance position, step forward strike with your knee. Your toes are pointing down. (pic 86)
- Take a step forward with your Front Leg.
- Push off the *Back-Leg* and bend your knee. (pic 88)
- Stretch your Back Leg towards your opponent while thrusting your hip and leaning back slightly.
- Weight is on the supporting leg.
- One hand is extending on delivery of the push kick, while the other hand is in guard position.
- Return to the original stance.

88	89	90

A similar technique is used for the Lead Leg push kick. This kick needs to be fast, to fend off your opponent or disrupt his rhythm and offence. (pics 91-93)

91	92	93

Bag Work

Practice striking and kicking technique on a bag. Pay attention to your technique (feet, legs, body, arms and fists) first before you start adding speed and power. You should include bag work practice in your routine (as demonstrated by Harald below)

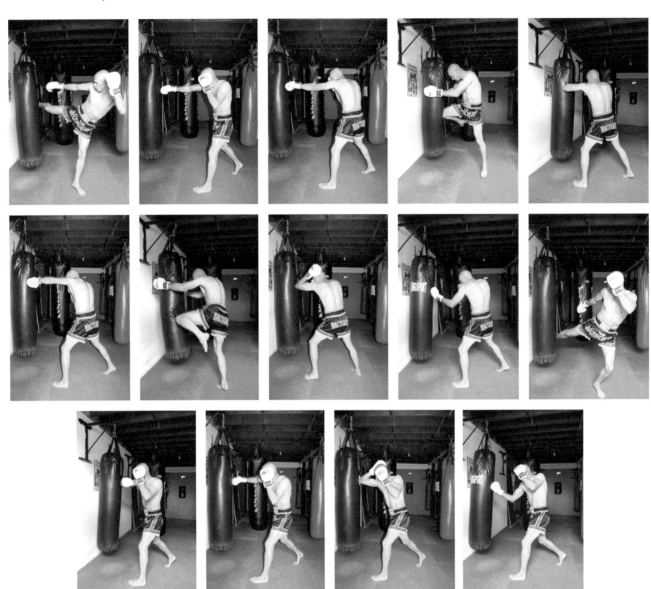

CHAPTER III

SLIPPING AND BLOCKING PUNCHES

<u>Slipping to avoid your opponent's left jab</u>

Different slipping techniques are used by different fighters. However, the fundamentals of the technique are similar.

- To slip a *Left Jab* of your opponent, your upper body slightly twists towards your right side. (pic 94)
- It should be just a small movement for better balance and countering possibilities.
- Some fighters also transfer body weight to the *Back Foot*.

94   95

A similar movement is used for slipping the right cross, but your body weight is transferred to the Front Foot. (pic 96)

96   97

Tip:

- The point of the slip is to counter with different strikes.
- Practice in front of the mirror.
- Practice slipping against your partner.

CHAPTER IV

BLOCKING/PARRYING
PUNCHES AND KICKS

You can use your palms to block/parry and use it to counter your opponent's Jabs and crosses.

100	101
Parrying jab	Parrying cross

You can also block hooks with your gloves by compacting them against your temple. Keep them strong to avoid being hit with your own palm or fist.

102	103
Blocking Jab	Blocking cross

To protect yourself from a hook you can use your fists, elbows, biceps and shoulders.

104

Blocking Left Hook

105

Blocking Right Hook

106

Blocking Left Hook

107

Blocking Right Hook

108

Blocking Right Uppercut

109

Blocking Left Uppercut

Blocking body kicks

When blocking a kick to your body, raise your knee to your elbow to form a shield. Point your shin towards the kick.

110 111

Dutch Style Blocking Body Kick. This type of defence enables you to follow with counters and combos

112

Blocking low kick

Raise your knee (just enough to block) in the direction of the kick (10 or 2 o'clock). The aim is to block a Low Kick with your shin.

115   116

Catching and controlling the push kick

1. Lean back from your opponent's push kick.
2. Simultaneously catch your opponent's foot with one palm. For stronger control of your opponent's leg, you may keep another palm over the foot. Use your hands to redirect the kick towards right or left.
3. Hold and lift the leg.
4. Keep your head back and out of reach of his arms. From that position, there are many possibilities for counters.

117

118

CHAPTER V

STRENGTH AND CONDITIONING

Below are some exercises that may help you to devise your training:

Neck

a) This exercise should be practiced with a partner. Grab your partner's head moving it down with your partner's resistance. Then your partner moves his head up with your resistance. Repeat 5-10 times each. Do not use too much resistance at the start. Please be careful when attempting to do any neck exercises.

120

121

Shoulders

1. Battle Ropes (3 sets for 1 minute). (pic 122)
2. Push ups – (wide).
3. Push ups –(narrow -old style Muay Thai). For triceps and arm strength

4. High intensity superset combination of small weights (dumbbells). Each set follows the next one without a break.

- Punching (30 sec). (Pic 125 -127)
- Lateral lift (30 sec). (Pic 131-132)
- Shoulder press (30 sec). (Pic 128-130)
- Lifting dumbbells with straight arms (30 sec). (Pic 133-134)
- Back to punching (30 sec).
- Shoulder press again (30 sec).

128   129   130

131   132

133   134

5. Chin ups

Legs

It is beneficial for a beginner to add leg strengthening exercises to develop your ability to move easily in the ring and generate a kicking power.

The following exercises should be included in your weekly training: skipping, jumping, lunges, wall-sits, running and sprinting. You can use them as compacting exercises (putting exercises together) or as supersets.

Many beginners ask whether there are any ways to condition ones' shins. Well, the toughening of your shins occurs naturally with small bumps and bruises or impacts (heavy bags or training) that calcify your shins and make it tougher and less sensitive.

1. Skipping
2. Running
3. Kicking against pads or bag
4. Lunges (3 sets x 15-20 reps)

<u>Leg Strength Routine</u>

135   136

5. Squats
6. Stairs climbing
7. Ring jumps

Core

1. Use different Ab exercise including planking.
2. Plank (3 minutes with a minute in each position as demonstrated below)

137

138

139

CHAPTER VI
HOW TO HOLD PADS

When you hold pads, meet the punch or the kick

HOLDING PADS FOR A JAB & CROSS

HOLDING PADS FOR a HOOK

HOLDING PADS FOR UPPERCUTS

148

149

HOLDING PADS FOR LOW KICKS

150

151

HOLDING PADS FOR A KNEW STRIKE

152

153

154

155

HOLDING PADS FOR PUSH KICKS

156

WHAT WE HAVE COVERED

<u>Warm up</u>

Before training your warm up routine may include the following:

1. Running 1-2 km depending on your level of running fitness
2. Skipping rope in 2x2 minutes rounds
3. Stretching
4. Shadow boxing working on your form
5. Combos on pads followed up by a bag work
6. Depending on your level and the advice of your coach you can also add sparring.

You can also watch a skilled fighter you like and learn his technique, movement and combinations. First, apply it in shadow boxing then practice it on a bag. Finally, include it in your sparring. It will take time to perfect the technique but as you grow in your experience and confidence it will become yours.

<u>Basic combos and movement</u>

1. Jab-Cross
2. Jab-cross- upper cut
3. Jab -Low kick
4. Jab – Body kick
5. Jab-Cross -Low Kick
6. Jab—cross - Low Kick – Body Kick
7. Jab-Cross-R Knee-R kick
8. Jab-cross- L Hook- Low kick
9. Four straight punches followed by R Elbow-R knee -R body kick

<u>Strength and conditioning as in chapter V</u>

<u>Holding Pads for your partner</u>

<u>What Your Need for Your First Training Session</u>

Comfortable sporting clothing, towel and a water bottle. Gyms usually provide gloves and other gear for your training. If you want to purchase your own gear, seek advice from your coach.

MESSAGE FROM OLI AND HARALD

Thank you for purchasing this book.

Learning Muay Thai can be a great journey. We are happy to share with you what we have learnt from legendary fighters in Asia, Europe and Australia. We would like to thank our students, friends and family who have and still share with us our Muay Thai journey.

We hope that by sharing our experiences with you we have planted a seed of growth and joy in your journey to self-discovery.

Enjoy

9227 7727
saslocksmiths.com

Printed in the United States
By Bookmasters